Etching on Birch Bark
Museum of the American Indian
Photograph by Alfred H. Tamarin

Ancient Deer Mask
University Museum, Philadelphia

HARPER & ROW, Publishers

NEW YORK, EVANSTON & LONDON

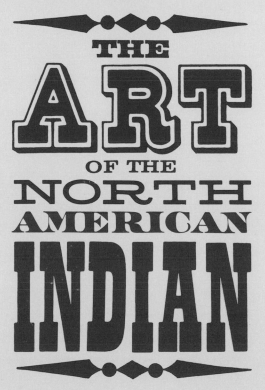

THE ART OF THE NORTH AMERICAN INDIAN

SHIRLEY GLUBOK

DESIGNED BY
OSCAR KRAUSS

THE AUTHOR GRATEFULLY ACKNOWLEDGES THE ASSISTANCE OF:
ELLEN MALINO, lecturer American History, The New School for Social Research
BARBARA GARRISON of The Spence School, New York
ALFRED H. TAMARIN
SAMUEL P. PEABODY of Rye Country Day School
MERVIN BLOCK of CBS News
ALEX J. WEINSTEIN of Ednalite Research Company
MONIQUE and ERIC BREINDEL

•

AND ESPECIALLY THE HELPFUL COOPERATION OF:
FREDERICK J. DOCKSTADER,
Director of the Museum of the American Indian, Heye Foundation

•

To the memory of
OLIVER LA FARGE

When Christopher Columbus landed in America, he found people with shining dark eyes, straight black hair, and copper-red skin. Columbus called these people "Indians" because he thought he had come upon India. These New World Indians were the first Americans.

The Indians of the United States and Canada belonged to tribes which were very different from one another. They lived and worked in many different ways. They spoke many different languages.

They all loved the sky, the seas, the mountains, the forests, and the animals that lived in them. They all used the materials they found in nature for their art. They made beautiful works of art from wood, sand, seashells, porcupine quills, and birch bark. Most North American Indian art honored their gods and spirits. Some of the art showed the brave deeds of the chiefs and warriors.

The Indian tribes of North America had many different ceremonies to honor their gods and spirits. They sang and danced. They shook rattles and beat tom-toms. Masks of all sorts played an important part in the ceremonies.

This wooden mask was made by Nootka Indians, who lived on Vancouver Island off the Pacific coast of Canada. The mask represents a wild man of the mountains. It was worn during midwinter dances. The dancer jumped around wildly. He would break away from the other dancers and rush about destroying property.

The mask is trimmed with hair made of strips of bark from a cedar tree. The eyebrows are made of fur, to make the face look even wilder.

Chicago Natural
History Museum

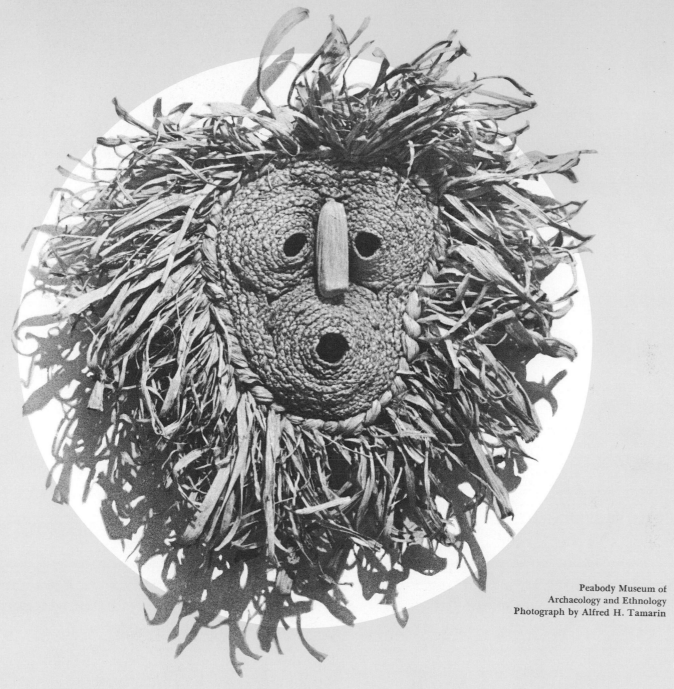

This mask was made from corn husks by the Senecas in New York State. Strips of corn husk are braided and wound into coils to make the shape of a face. Members of the Husk Face Society were also known as "Bushyheads." They wore corn-husk masks in hopes of getting good crops.

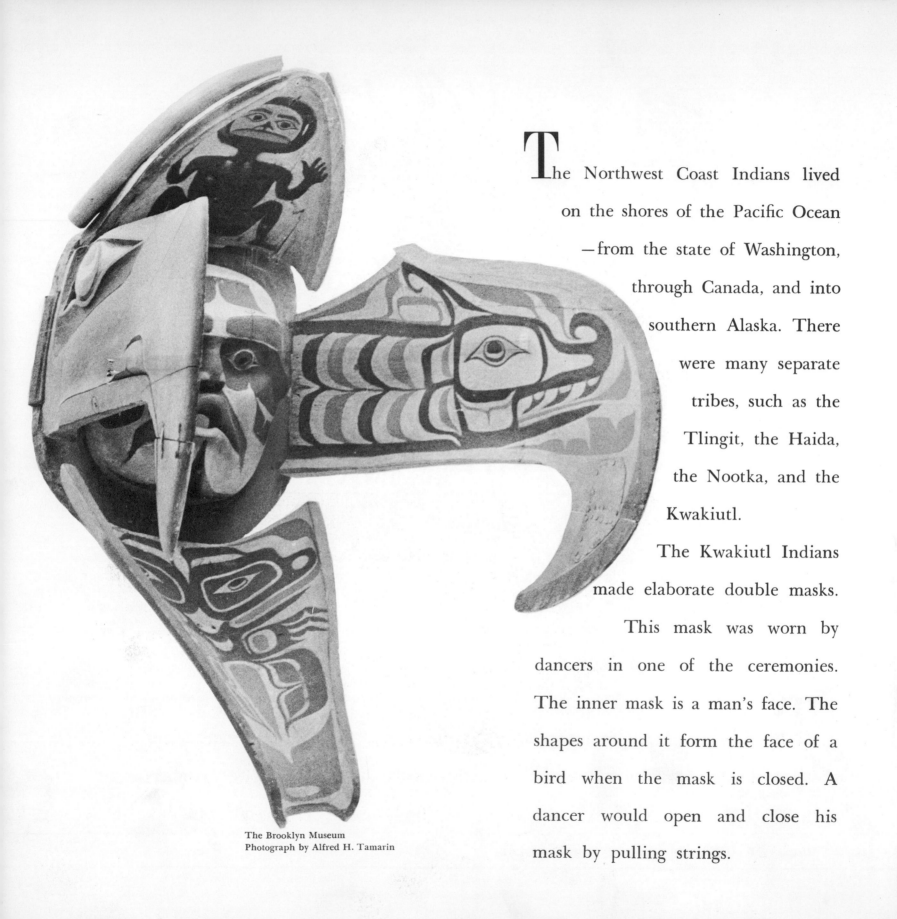

The Northwest Coast Indians lived on the shores of the Pacific Ocean —from the state of Washington, through Canada, and into southern Alaska. There were many separate tribes, such as the Tlingit, the Haida, the Nootka, and the Kwakiutl.

The Kwakiutl Indians made elaborate double masks. This mask was worn by dancers in one of the ceremonies. The inner mask is a man's face. The shapes around it form the face of a bird when the mask is closed. A dancer would open and close his mask by pulling strings.

The wood mask above was made by the Tlingit Indians. It has a strange-looking face, with teeth made of shell. Otters, little furry animals, are carved on its cheeks and forehead. This mask was worn by medicine men.

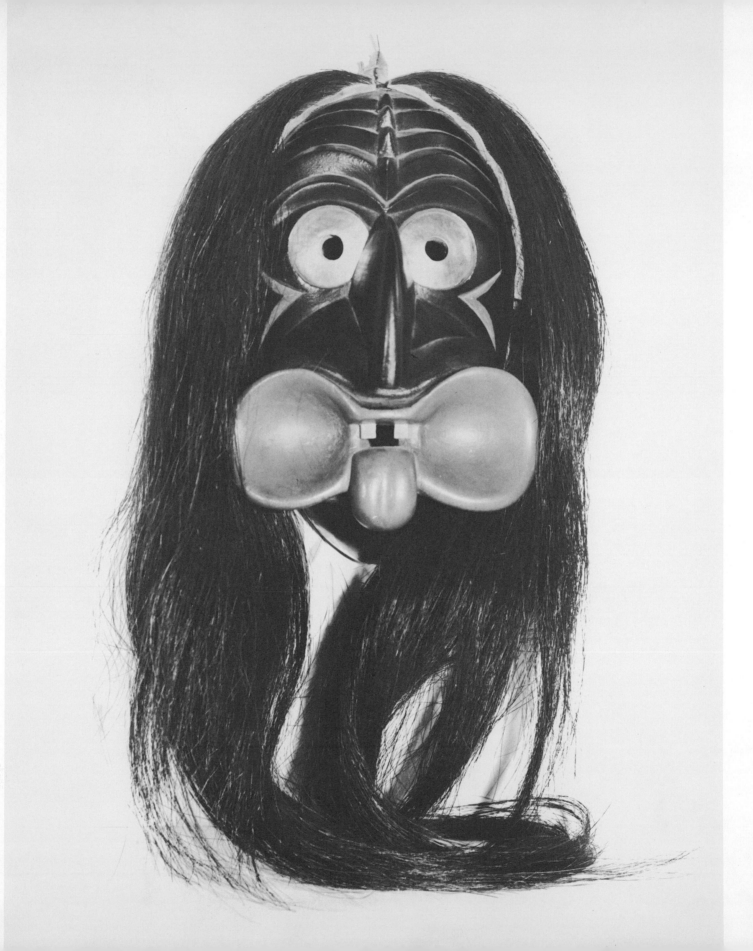

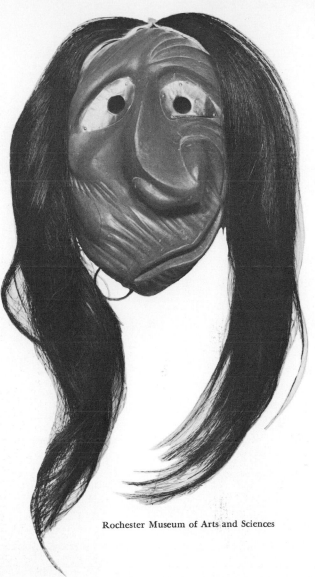

The Iroquois believed that evil spirits caused
illness. Members of their False Face societies wore masks
to drive away the evil spirits and cure the sick.

They carved these masks from living trees in the forest.
This kept the masks "alive" and saved their magic powers.

After a three-day ceremony of singing and dancing,
the Iroquois carver went into the forest to choose a tree.
He usually burned tobacco leaves to honor the spirit
of the living tree. He made a quick carving of the mask
in the tree. He cut his mask out. Then he took
it home to finish it.

If the mask was cut out of the tree in the morning, it was
painted red. If it was cut out in the afternoon,
the mask was painted black.

These False Face masks are bold and startling. The eyes
are rimmed with metal that glowed in the light of the campfire.
The wigs are made from the hairs of a horse's tail.

Rochester Museum of Arts and Sciences

The tall trees in the northern forests provided huge supplies of wood. The big trees suggested big wooden carvings.

This unusual wood carving of a man lying on his back is a giant-sized bowl, called a *potlatch* bowl. It is carved from a single log. It is almost as big as a canoe. The body and head are hollowed out to make bowls. The face is a lid. Two smaller bowls rest on the knees, and there are extra bowls beside the figure.

The potlatch bowl was filled with such foods as salmon with candlefish oil or seal blubber with berries. It was used in an unusual ceremony by the Kwakiutl tribe. For special events, such as marriages or the raising of a totem pole, a splendid feast was held, called a potlatch. There was much boastful speech-making. There was chanting and dancing. The host gave away valuable gifts, to show off. But he knew that he would receive even greater gifts at a later potlatch.

Fine old wood carvings were made in Florida. This graceful cat statue is over five hundred years old. The cat seems to be kneeling on human legs.

The statue was carved with tools of sharpened seashells and sharks' teeth. Indians did not have iron or steel tools until Europeans settled in America.

On the Northwest coast the Indians lived in houses built of giant cedar logs. Giant cedar totem poles stood in front of the houses of the chiefs and other important members of the tribe.

These Indians believed that their great-grandfathers and great-great-grandfathers had been animals, fish, and birds, as well as men. The totem pole told the story of these ancestors.

Totem poles were carved with figures of people and animals, squatting in unusual positions. The figures were carved one on top of the other to fit the shape of the pole. Totem pole artists were very important members of the tribe.

This figure is the base of a totem pole made by the Haida Indians. It shows a hunter and a beaver. The whole totem pole is forty-three feet, five inches tall. It weighs four thousand four hundred and ninety pounds. Totem poles are the tallest wood carvings in the world.

Museum of the American Indian
Photograph by Carmelo G. Guadagno

Huge sea-going canoes were also made from the great cedars in the Northwest. The cedar logs were hollowed out to make boats for fighting and fishing. This Tlingit figure of a man was on the prow of a canoe to guide it safely through the water. Its eyes and teeth are shell. Human hair is glued onto its head.

Museum of the American Indian   Photograph by Carmelo G. Guadagno

A Salish tribe on the Northwest coast was nick-named the "Flatheads." The wood carving on the left shows a mother and her papoose. The baby's head is wrapped to flatten it.

Basketmaking is perhaps the oldest Indian art. Indian baskets of all shapes and sizes were used for storing, carrying, and cooking. The Indians cooked food in watertight baskets. They heated rocks and dropped them into the water to make it boil. The Apache basket above is large enough to hold a man. It was used for storage. The color for the basket designs came from roots and bark. The small Tlingit basket below is decorated with killer whales.

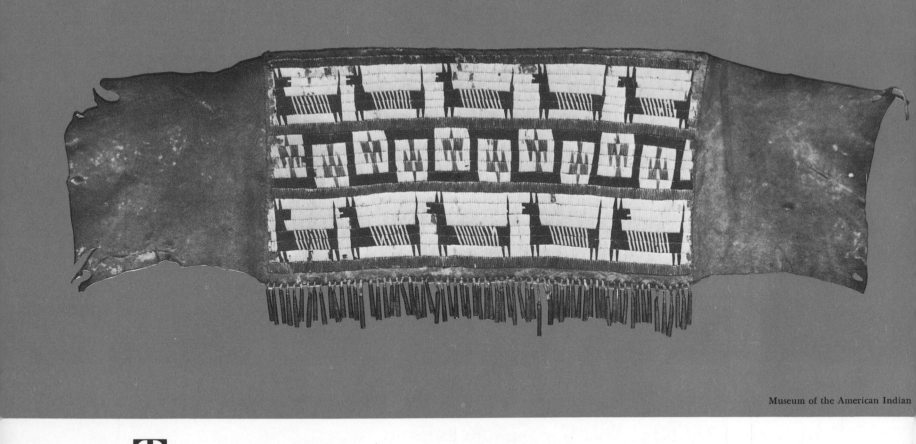

The North American Indians were the only people in the world to use the prickly quills of the porcupine to make beautiful designs. First the Indians broke off the sharp points of the quills. Then they softened the quills with water and flattened them. They colored them with dyes made from plants. The Indians sewed the porcupine quills on soft animal skins, such as deerskin.

Above is a leather cradle cover for a Delaware Indian papoose. The simple figures were made with straight lines. The fine buckskin moccasins also were decorated with porcupine quills.

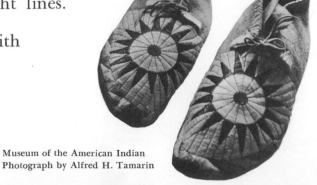

The Europeans who settled in America sold glass beads to the Indians. The beads became more popular than porcupine quills. The Indians loved the bright colors of the glass beads. They could make curved lines with the beads. This vest is embroidered with two Dakota Indians on horseback, holding American flags.

The turtle shows a wonderful design the Indians made with colored beads. The beads were strung on threads to make a mosaic pattern that covers the whole turtle. The turtle is a charm, which was believed to bring long life to a newly born Indian papoose.

Museum of the American Indian
Photograph by Alfred H. Tamarin

Wampum is the name for strings of polished beads made from the hard shell of the quahog clam. The shell beads were woven into designs.

The Indians used designs in wampum as records of important events. This "belt" tells of a group of Western Chippewa chiefs who visited King George III in England in 1807. Whenever chiefs met for important ceremonies, they displayed belts of wampum.

Wampum was difficult to make with the simple tools of the Indians. So the beads were scarce. They became valuable, and the early Dutch settlers began to use wampum beads as money. The

purple beads were worth more than the white ones because most of the clam shell is white and only a tiny bit of each shell is purple. Wampum was the first money used for business with the Indians. It was also used by the Dutch and English to trade among themselves.

The Zuni and Hopi tribes
of New Mexico and Arizona believed in
Kachinas. Kachinas were a
tribe of good spirits. They were
supposed to visit the
Indian villages and help the people.

Zuni and Hopi Indian dancers
put on masks and believed that they
themselves became Kachinas.
They danced and feasted in ceremonies
that lasted from sunrise to
sunset. The land in the Southwest
is very dry. Kachina dancers prayed
for rain to water the crops.

The Brooklyn Museum
Photographs by Alfred H. Tama

The dancers gave Kachina dolls to children as gifts.
The children took them home to remind them of the friendly spirits.

Kachina dolls are carved from the soft cottonwood tree. The
clothes and masks on the dolls are copies of those worn
by Kachina dancers. The Zuni dolls wear costumes made of cloth and
feathers. The costumes of the Hopi dolls are painted on the wood.

There are different dolls for different dances. The one at
the far left is a Hilili Kachina doing a dance with a snake. The
Kweywu dolls riding piggyback are clowns.

At the right is a Paiyakyamu clown. His body is painted in black
and white stripes, and he has horns. He is a glutton, one
who eats too much.

The Yuma Indians of Arizona made dolls of clay for children to play with. The artists baked the clay in open ovens to make the dolls hard. They are carefully made to look like people, with ten fingers and ten toes.

The little dolls were
dressed in tiny copies
of the clothes and jewelry
worn by the Indians.
Their faces and bodies were
painted to look tattooed.
The dolls are lovable
with their wide, staring eyes
and flowing hair.

Millions of buffalo once roamed the Great Plains. The skins of the buffalo were used to make robes, tepee covers, shields, leggings, moccasins, and many other things.

This is a buffalo-skin robe. It is painted with a scene of a raid on an enemy camp to capture horses. All of the horses are painted from the side. They are all the same size, yet the figures near the top are supposed to be farther away than the figures at the bottom. The Indian artist showed one group of captured horses by painting just the heads.

When the proud Cheyenne chief wrapped himself in this robe and walked around, the horses seemed to move.

The Indians loved paintings of hunting and battle scenes. Paints were made from minerals and plants. A gluey substance was used to make the colors stick to the hide. This glue was sometimes made by boiling the tail of a beaver. Brushes were made from the spongy knee bone of a buffalo, or from horn or sticks or animal hairs.

In later years Indians began to use paper, pencils, and crayons that they got from European settlers. This sketch was made in a notebook by a Dakota Indian. It looks like the picture on the hide painting. It shows a man on horseback fighting an enemy. There are many little lines, or details, in this sketch which are not found in hide paintings. These details are difficult to paint on hides but easy to make with pencil and pen.

Indians of North America had never seen horses until Spanish settlers brought them from Europe.

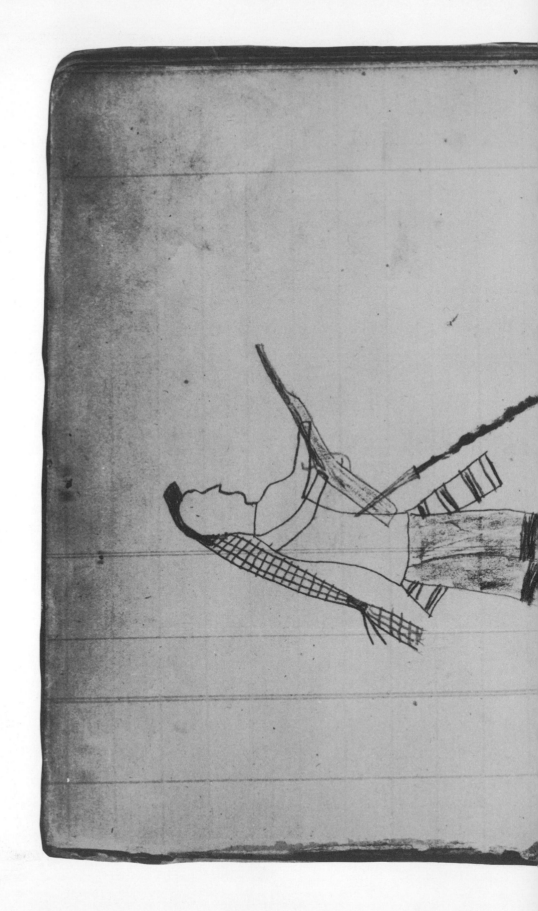

As time went on, Indian artists learned to use other modern materials, such as watercolors. The painting on the left shows fun-making clowns, called Koshares.

The Navajos of the Southwest made sand paintings by dropping fine grains of colored sand onto a bed of natural sand. The designs usually showed Navajo gods and the wonders of nature.

Sand paintings were part of magic healing ceremonies. The sand painting on the right was used to try to heal someone struck by lightning or injured in a storm. It shows Big Thunder with a birdlike body and feet of clouds. Rainspouts hang from the wings. The arrows stand for lightning. Sand paintings were begun in the morning. They had to be finished and destroyed before sunset of the same day. This design is a small part saved from a large sand painting.

Museum of the American Indian

Indian pottery makers shaped their pots by hand. The bowl above is about eight hundred years old. It was found in the grave of a Mimbres Indian in the Southwest. The figure on the bowl is part mountain lion and part human. The hole was made to let the spirit of the figure escape and travel with its owner.

The animal-shaped pot below also was made long before Columbus by the *Anasazi,* or "ancient ones."

On the right is a Mohave clay jar with four spouts and a human head decorated with strings of colored beads.

Museum of the American Indian
Photograph by Carmelo G. Guadagno

Rasmussen Collection
Portland Art Museum

This unusual coat was worn on important occasions by Tlingit Indians. The design shows brown bears. The coat is made of goat's wool and cedar bark. The cedar bark was first soaked in salt water and then beaten with a whale-bone mallet. The sleeves of the coat were made of woolen yarn, and the coat was trimmed with otter fur. Extra otter fur was added at the sides of the coat.

The Navajo Indians wove blankets from the wool of wild mountain goats. The wool was colored with dyes made from charcoal, plants, and berries. Later, when the Spaniards brought sheep to America, sheep's wool was used. This Navajo blanket has a pattern of birds perched on Corn Gods. Navajo blankets were worn by Indians many years ago. Nowadays the blankets are also used as rugs.

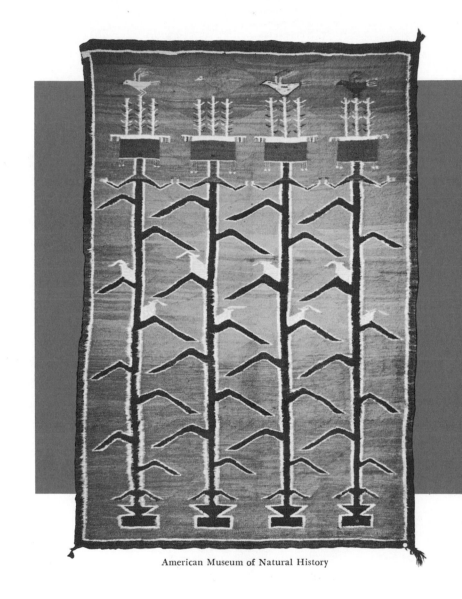

American Museum of Natural History

Smithsonian Institution

Robert and Lisa Sainsbury Collection, London
Photograph Museum of Primitive Art: Charles Uht

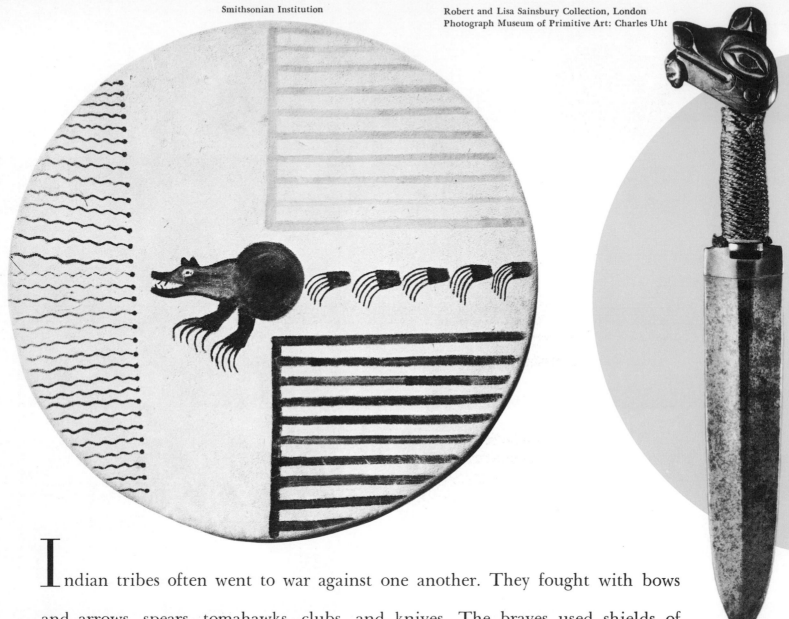

Indian tribes often went to war against one another. They fought with bows and arrows, spears, tomahawks, clubs, and knives. The braves used shields of tough buffalo hide. The shields were painted with magic pictures to protect and identify the warrior. This Crow Indian shield shows a charging bear.

Indians sometimes made knives with steel they found in wrecked ships. This fighting knife from Canada is thought to be Haida. The handle, in the shape of an animal, is carved of wood.

This Chippewa war club was carved in the shape of a bird's head with a ball in its beak. It is solid wood. It was carved around 1900, following an old tomahawk design. Most tomahawks were carved more simply than this one.

The shield cover above is painted with an exciting battle scene. It shows a fight between the Crows and the Sioux, both Indian tribes of the Great Plains. The Sioux chief in the center is wearing a feathered war bonnet. He carries a shield with a buffalo design.

Wooden helmets protected Indian warriors in battle. They were carved to frighten and fool the enemy. This Tlingit helmet shows a man's head with his face twisted in pain.

This helmet, also Tlingit, was worn in battle and in ceremonies. It is carved in the shape of an animal's head, with teeth of shell. The helmet is trimmed with copper and fur.

The Indians were the first people to smoke a leaf which we now call tobacco. They smoked it in pipes of many shapes and sizes. Some weighed as much as eighteen pounds. The finest pipes were carved from Ohio pipestone, fine-grained clay that is as hard as stone.

The stone statue on the left is a pipe found in Oklahoma. The tobacco went into a hole in the little man's back. The figure above is a wooden pipe. The pipe below is made of stone.

Carved pipes were used by tribes all over North America. Chiefs and warriors were proud of their pipes, and they handed them down to their sons.

The Indians used pipes for ceremonies, especially around the council fire. The peace pipe is famous in American history.

William Penn smoked the peace pipe with the Delaware Indians when he bought the land that is now southeastern Pennsylvania. The Pueblo Indians smoked pipes called cloud blowers, to call for rain.

On the left is a finely carved stone pipe showing a spoonbill duck seated on a fish. It is one of the finest pipes found in the Hopewell Mound in Ohio. It is four and a half inches long and two inches high.

The Wyandot pipe below shows Indian art in a playful mood. A man and a bear are fighting over a little barrel.

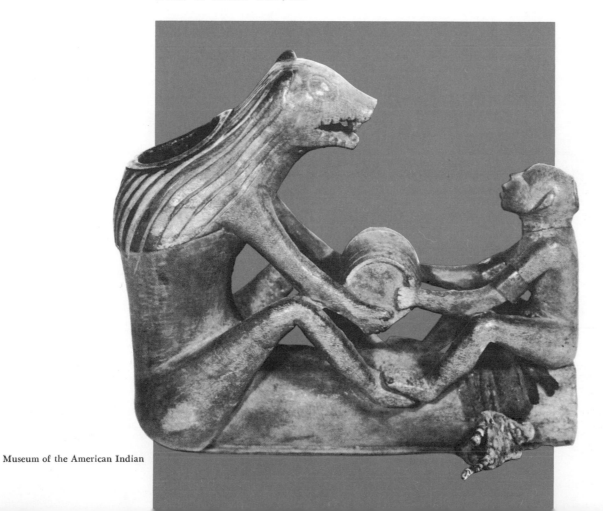

Museum of the American Indian

Indians combed their long dark hair with combs made of bone or wood. This comb was carved from red cedar wood by the Tlingits of the Northwest.

The forests in the Northeast were full of beautiful silver-birch trees. The Indians used birch bark to make wigwams, canoes, and other useful things.

Indian artists made pictures in birch bark. They scraped away the white outer layer of bark to form silhouette designs in the brown layer underneath. The birch-bark box at the right shows bears, beavers, and caribou (or reindeer). It was made by Cree Indians. The sides of the box are sewn together with roots from the spruce tree.

At the left is an ancient petroglyph, or rock carving. It is a stone scratched with drawings of a mountain sheep family. It came from a boulder in a canyon in California.

The carving above is Haida, from Queen Charlotte Islands, British Columbia. It is made of argillite, a soft stone often called slate. Argillite becomes shiny jet black after it has been rubbed and polished.

On the right is a carved Tlingit fishhook for catching huge halibut in the deep Pacific waters. The carvings were believed to have magic powers. This halibut hook is almost a foot long.

North American Indian art is many arts of many tribes. Some of it, such as totem poles, wampum, and porcupine-quill work, was known nowhere else in the world.

Indian art in the United States and Canada began long before Columbus. It continued through all the hard years of exploration and growth. Today some of the older tribesmen still weave blankets and make pottery just as their ancestors did hundreds of years ago.

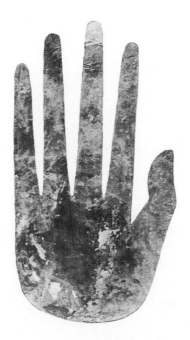

Ancient Mica Hand
Chicago Natural History Museum

709.7
GLU
GLUBOK, SHIRLEY
  The art of the North
American Indian

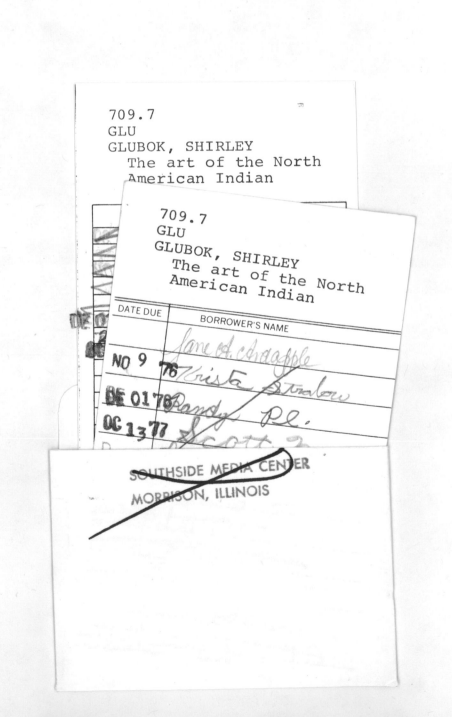

709.7
GLU
GLUBOK, SHIRLEY
  The art of the North
American Indian

DATE DUE	BORROWER'S NAME
	Jane A. Chaapple
NO 9 76	Krista Strabow
DE 01 76	Randy Pl.
OC 13 77	Scott 3